BICYCLE SAFETY

Printed in the United States of America.

Library of Congress Cataloging-in-Publication Data
Loewen, Nancy, 1964–
Bicycle safety / Nancy Loewen.
p.   cm.
Includes bibliographical references.
Summary: Explains the safe way to ride a bicycle and
identifies such important equipment as the helmet,
reflectors, and basket.
ISBN 1-56766-260-9 (hardcover : lib. bdg.)
1. Cycling—Safety measures—Juvenile literagure.
2. Bicycles—Safety measures—Juvenile literature
[1. Bicycles and bicycling—Safety measures.   2. Safety.]
I. Title.
GV1055.L64   1996
796.6'028'9--dc20   95-45042
CIP
AC

BICYCLE SAFETY

By Nancy Loewen   Illustrated by Penny Dann

THE CHILD'S WORLD

Riding your bike can be a lot of fun. But it's also serious business. Pickles and Roy will show you what to do—and what not to do—to ride your bike safely!

A bike is a vehicle, just like a car or truck. When you get on a bike you become a driver. To be a good, safe driver, you need to know and follow the rules of the road. These rules will help **prevent** you from getting hurt, or from hurting others.

Bicycle safety begins before you even get on your bike. First, make sure your bike is the right size for you. You should be able to sit on the seat and touch the ground with the tips of your toes. If your bike is too big or too small, you won't be able to control it very well—and that means trouble!

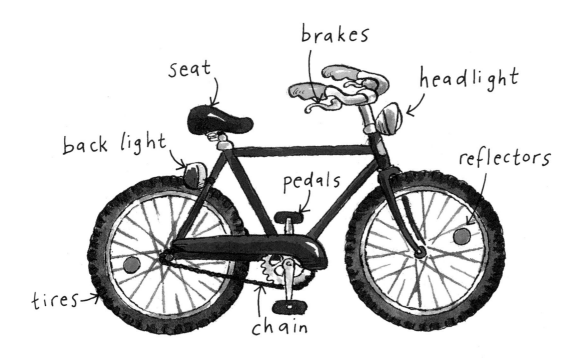

brakes

seat

headlight

back light

reflectors

pedals

tires→

chain

Next, make sure that your bike has all the
equipment it needs, and that everything works.

You need a special piece of equipment, too. Always wear a helmet when bicycling. The helmet should fit straight on your head and cover half of your forehead. It should be snug, not loose.

Some kids think it's not cool to wear a helmet. But remember, professional **cyclists** wear helmets all the time, and they're definitely cool!

Floppy pant legs or loose shoelaces can cut your trip short if they get caught in your bike chain. Wear pants that have close-fitting legs, and keep your shoe laces tied.

Learn all the bike safety rules, and show your parents that you know them, before riding your bike in the street. Practice riding safely on sidewalks, driveways, or bike paths.

On the street, always ride with traffic, on the right side of the road. Keep as close to the curb as possible, and ride single file.

Be alert! Watch out for **pedestrians**, potholes, **sewer grates**, parked cars, and anything else that might get in your way.

Always obey traffic **signals** and signs.

Before crossing a street, stop and look left, right, and left again to make sure there's no traffic.

left   right   left again

If you don't think you can make it across without hurrying, wait until you can. At busy **intersections**, walk your bike across instead of riding it.

Don't forget to check for traffic when entering a street from a driveway, parking lot, alley, or sidewalk.

Use hand signals to show others where you're going.

Always have both hands on the handlebars except when signaling. If you need to carry something, use a basket or backpack.

When braking, apply equal **pressure** to the front and rear brakes. If you brake suddenly with the front brake, you might be thrown over the handlebars. And if you brake suddenly with the rear brake, your bike might skid out of control.

Be aware of changing conditions. Your brakes won't work as well in the rain or on loose gravel or sand, so brake gently and allow plenty of time to come to a stop.

It's best not to ride your bike at night. If you have to, though, wear light-colored clothes so others can see you easily. Putting **reflective** tape on your bike, helmet, shoes, or clothes is a good idea, too.

These rules might seem like a lot to remember. But they're very important, so do your best to learn them. Practice them every time you get on your bike. Be a safe cyclist, not a sorry one!

Glossary

cyclists (SI-klests)
those who ride a cycle. Professional
cyclists wear helmets all the time.

intersections (in-ter-SEK-shens)
where two or more streets cross.
Walk your bike across intersections
instead of riding it.

pedestrians (pe-DES-tre-ans)
people moving on foot. Watch for pedestrians walking in crosswalks.

pressure (PRE-sher)
the act of pressing or pushing. Apply
equal pressure to front and rear brakes
when stopping.

prevent (pre -VENT)
to act ahead of; to keep from happening.
These rules will help prevent you from
getting hurt.

sewer grates (SU-er GRATS)
a frame of iron bars, found in the streets,
for rain water to go underground. While
riding your bike, watch out for sewer
grates that might get in your way.

signals (SIG-nels)
a sign or action that tells others what is
going to happen. Use hand signals to let
others know where you are going.

reflective (re-FLEK-tiv)
capable of bending back light.
Reflective tape on your bike, helmet,
shoes, or clothes helps others see
you better at night.

DATE			

mv